SONGS
IN THE
NIGHT

Christian Pascale

Aster Press
Blue Fortune Enterprises, LLC

SONGS IN THE NIGHT

Copyright © 2022 Christian Pascale, Pascale Living Trust

All rights reserved. Printed in the United States of America. No part of this book may be used or reproduced in any manner whatsoever without written permission except in the case of brief quotations embodied in critical articles or reviews.

This book is a work of fiction. Names, characters, businesses, organizations, places, events and incidents either are the product of the author's imagination or are used fictitiously. Any resemblance to actual persons, living or dead, events, or locales is entirely coincidental.

For information contact :
Blue Fortune Enterprises, LLC
Aster Press
P.O. Box 554
Yorktown, VA 23690
http://blue-fortune.com

Interior and Cover design by Blue Fortune Enterprises LLC,
blue-fortune.com
Cover art by Liria Pascale

ISBN: 978-1-948979-93-1
First Edition: January 2023

Dedication

To my wife Liria and my two sons, Raphael and Michel.

Other Titles by Christian Pascale:

Memories are the Stories We Tell Ourselves
Windows of Heaven
Poetry of Wonder

Editor's Note

Dear Reader,

As a writer, Christian Pascale's strength was in his poetry. He took the feelings he had about life, love, and God and molded words around those feelings. He was a gentle soul who loved greatly.

I received a text from Chris once. It was inspirational and moving and wonderful, and I texted back a sincere thank you. "Oh, sorry," he said. "That wasn't for you." When I was done laughing (because honestly, does it matter where the inspiration comes from or whether it was meant for you or not?) I asked him who it was meant for. "My son," he said.

Father, husband, poet, novelist... Chris lived each role fully.

He approached life with a zeal for adventure, learning, and connecting with others. In his first book, *Memories Are The Stories We Tell Ourselves*, he says in the preface, "I believe that writing is a way of communication with the wider world and a means to transmit something of what we have experienced. Each new experience contributes to who we are, and I would not be who I am without having lived and loved and met such a wide variety of characters."

A graduate of Lafayette College and American University, Chris loved to travel. When he was in his twenties, he lived in France where he taught tennis (which he enjoyed playing throughout his life) while working on his Doctorate in contemporary French history at the Sorbonne. Later in life, Chris worked for the government in a career that would take him to foreign countries where there was great unrest.

A kind and gentle soul, Chris had a quiet sense of humor and an enduring love of family. His pride in his two sons, Raphael and Michel, was evident whenever he spoke of them, and his love for his wife, Liria, was profound.

We all miss him greatly, but we are also grateful for the words he left us.

Narielle Living
Editor

PROLOGUE

Poems are like gemstones. The more they're polished, the clearer they shine.

Many of these poems were written for adults. Several were written for children. I included them because they speak to the child in all of us. Poetry is about hiding complexity inside simplicity.

Readers have said that this fresh, human, and realistic set of poems flows from page to page and is entertaining, humorous, hopeful and thought provoking.

I hope you enjoy them.

Christian

Bird in a Cage

Like a bird locked in a cage
my heart longs to fly away.
It wonders what it's like to fly
to stretch its wings and reach the sky.

No bars, no cage of doubt and fear.
Unfettered vision from on high
but can it turn the tattered page
and win its freedom from this cage?

This prison in my head
cripples wings made to fly.
Caught in a web of memories
if I could only catch the breeze

and ride the future's smooth updraft
to find a freedom that will last.
To leave this prison far behind
and touch the world my heart will find.

Conversation

I love the time we spent today
the way the conversation flowed.
It would have it no other way.
I saw your face, it glowed.

Now you're gone and I'm alone,
the sun has set, the day is gone,
and I would give all that I own
to see you once before the dawn.

And in the darkness of this night
I let my mind find dreams of you.
But should these dreams grow dark, take flight,
I do not know what I would do.

Blessed

I want to see a burst of light
shining within my darkest night,
hear God's voice, majestic and loud
roar above life's deafening crowd.

But you spoke quiet, soft as air
not in my way with pomp and flare.
"Be still and know. My will is done,
for I am all, the perfect One."

And when I took that simple path
and looked for You in every task
made everything to You a prayer,
I found Your Love was everywhere.

Cabin in the Woods (Homage to Robert Frost)

The woods I see amidst the snow
hide a small cabin far below.
Though hidden, I know it's there.
A wisp of smoke floats on the air.

The day is cold, grows colder still.
I plunge through woods covered in snow.
The smell of burning wood grows clear.
I know my haven is very near.

No footprints there to lead the way.
They all have gone with yesterday.
But my hound dog, faithful guide
leads me down the steep hillside

The two of us shake off the snow
The cabin's owner, who I know,
provides hot soup to cut the chill
revive my soul, strengthen my will.

He says to me, "Then stay a while.
The nearest road's more than a mile.
Tomorrow the storm will break
And we could fish down by the lake."

The fire in the hearth burns bright.
It tempts me with its warmth and light.
I've commitments, places to go
though the fire pulls me with its glow.

Letter To Us All
(Fifty years ago)

Dear Friend,
If I could return to one important date,
I think it would be June six of 1968.
It was still not too late.

We believed in justice.
He gave us hope we could make a new world
with flag of truth unfurled.

Bobby said we'd stand tall,
as a nation we wouldn't fall
but move forward with equity for all.

No more war, no more hate.
Until that awful date
it was still not too late.

We heard the mournful knell
Didn't ask why or for whom sounded the bell.
It tolled for us as well.
Remember what our world could have been.

Colors of Light

The colors of rainbows are six.
We often see the colors mix
in richer shades diversified
like our world when unified.

Not just the red, not just the blue
we share all colors through and through.
Like graceful sky-arcs we shine bright,
reflecting colors of the light.

We're paintings using all light's colors
each one different from the others.
Heaven's portrait is what we see
when we reflect life's radiancy.

Courage and Confidence

Don't listen to doubting whispers
that take away your confidence.
Or their put-down, shouting sisters
which make the strongest of us wince.

The lies they tell are all the same.
Give up, give-in, you cannot win.
That is the nature of their game.
Don't stop and take it on the chin.

For lies are simply not the Truth.
You know just who you are.
Your courage is not plucked like fruit
nor bottled in a jelly jar.

It is a force, a mental strength
that comes from deep within.
It brings you victory at length
and lets new life begin.

Estranged Intelligence

Come taste Eden's apple,
eat those of Avalon.
Climb tower of Babel,
touch sky with upturned palm.

Come fly with Icarus
to seek the Truth's warm light.
With wings so close to the sun,
you fall in death's dark night.

You try to trick the gods,
Sisyphus lost in time.
Roll a rock up again
as penalty for some crime.

With fallen angel's pride
you tumble from the sky.
A dreamer searching time
who never finds out why.

Build your mighty temple
Or fly to heaven's seat.
Not in golden apples
the knowledge that you seek.

A Promise

I watched in horror from afar
as twin towers burned, crumbled, and fell.
People jumped, like glowing match sticks
flamed-out as they fell to the earth.

You called me, voiced your deep sorrow.
"Let's cancel our lunch," you said.
I said, "No, we must carry on."
At lunch as we shook hands, I felt

what you underlined in words.
"Ukraine stands behind the U.S."
Clear words, I knew you meant them.
Just like you know I mean this now.

As I see your cities crumble
and your children suffer,
I know your people will stand, fight
for country and for family.

If I were the man I once was
I would drop all, rush to your aid.
What I can only do is pray.
Bless the Ukraine and her people.

Fireflies

Fireflies light the sky
fireworks on fourth of July,
Normal celebration of life,
shows peace beyond all worldly strife.

Lightships sailing tides of night,
they blink their hope during flight
as if to say the day will come
when all this darkness will be done.

Flash of Gold

A hint of gold, a flash so bright
I see the goldfinch by day's light.
A spot of sun on a rainy day
enough to chase my clouds away.

A harbinger adorned in gold.
sign of prosperity foretold,
courage, wisdom, omen of good.
A sign of life now understood.

Fog

Fog creeps in on feline feet.
In silence covers school and street
and all the places that we meet
are cloaked in gray shroud or sheet.

The sun is gone, the light of day
all the children gone away.
It took them right where they lay
though all of us had hoped they'd stay.

As mist rises from the ground
their bloody bodies were all found,
Eerie quiet, the only sound
Of weeping parents all around.

Tomorrow brings another day
but can our sun keep fog away?
To this end we sit and pray
that we can keep the fog at bay.

Beaver Dam

When walking once in spring-draped land
I came upon a beaver dam.
Branches blocked water's downstream flow
from higher pond to woods below.

I focused on a floating leaf
trapped by the dam, a clear motif;
persistent, sought a passage through,
though stopped, it tried and tried anew.

Like stream of water, we can flow
and daily dams can never slow
our progress which will ever grow.
for movement is the way we show

our forward steps, avoid the rocks
of place or lack or aging clocks.
For Love is here and everywhere
and we are always in Her care.

For My Son

It's not wrong to live with a dream
though useless it may seem.
Dreams are what the heart's made of
And dreams often come from above.

The path that all the others walk
was not the path you chose or sought.
You can't be them; they can't be you.
We're not species in some zoo.

A day will come, not far from now
your dream you freely will avow.
It takes raw courage to pursue
the dream that is a part of you.

Ghost on the Beach

The foam rides in on somber waves.
Spreading its light on darker beach.
The bubbles look like snow white lace
now lit by moonbeams' hopeful reach.

The sand, wet with the night's embrace,
cools the hot passion of my thoughts.
Another time another place
just some memories I have sought.

I see her farther down the sand.
She bends, collects sea's lost jewels.
Another beach, another land,
she cups sand crabs from empty pools.

She seems to turn and look at me.
There is no better place to be
than walking gently by this sea.
Yet spectral image starts to flee

I wonder if she were a ghost,
A gossamer of what was there.
I think I miss her laugh the most.
It floated softly on the air.

Grace

God's grace shows us a perfect Love,
a gentle calm just like a dove
who nests in trust and fears no ill,
for Love eternal's with us still.

Grace shows me who and where I am,
So safe inside God's loving plan.
And in this grace, I understand
my neighbor as His perfect man.

When we feel God's loving grace
in every thought, in every place,
we meet our own, our neighbor's needs
for grace from God our pathway leads.

Gypsum Dunes

Martian walks on gypsum
dunes, the last of his kind.
Once wet and warm, now in ruins,
Mars resembles earth's cold moon.

Three billion years or more ago
airboats flew cross crystal seas
through the wetlands rivers flowed.
The loss of atmosphere the key

to disappearance of the seas.
Hesperian age came to an end.
Solar winds caused air to flee.
Then to earth's womb her life would send

on rocket wings the cargo flew.
Archean Age when life began.
From death of one the other grew.
Five million years, the rise of man.

The Martian walks on gypsum sand.
Remembers breeze on summer seas.
In dreams returns to former land's
forgotten images of trees.

Haven

It stands against the blowing sand.
amidst the howling wind, a light.
Life's lustrous blade in darkness shines
a wealth of warmth in cold of night.

Tattered traveler, lost, alone
seeks shelter from death's dark swarm.
In anguished searching a way home,
finds haven from time's raging storm.

Heaven in My Backyard

I look out my backyard window
and see a luminous yellow
like the color in a rainbow
set against a deep blue meadow.

It's the goldfinch in the morning.
Behind him the hydrangeas grow
blue like the summer sky's dawning
or the purple sun's setting glow.

God is a perfect artist
His painting's heaven I see.
A gift, His holy harvest
given to you and to me.

Her Room Upstairs

Your clothes are on the bed upstairs,
your bright red dress and underwear
laid out as for some grand event.

The room arranged like a shrine
to memories of what was mine.
Like the roses I once sent

so faded now, lost somehow
like laughter and our wedding vows.
The promised years we once spent.

This Spring I will unlock the door,
let in fresh air and sweep the floor,
and fix our bed that now is bent.

Perhaps fresh flowers from our yard
will somehow fix the room that's marred
by stale perfume's intrusive scent.

But if I took that scent away
your memory might never stay.
I'd live a life of discontent.

I think I'll leave things as they are
for one should never go too far
removing love's long-lost lament.

House on the Hill

The summer house was on a hill.
We were there but a week and still
some weeks can be seen as sublime
tapestries of passing time

woven with hours of emotions,
probing heights, depths like oceans
that ebb and flow throughout the soul
before the parts reveal a whole.

I am Here

"Why are we here, not there?"
Some ask with deep despair.
But I would call it Providence
To breathe this morning air.

In Your Blue Eyes

In your blue eyes, I see the splendor
of distant seas and cloud-free skies.
My heart's so full of wide-eyed wonder
at sapphire clouds within your eyes.

In your blue eyes, I see the splendor
of quiet rain on sandy beach,
of summer days and self-surrender
to something once beyond my reach.

In your blue eyes, I see the splendor
of dreams once shared and life we've made.
Within my heart, now much more tender
I find a truth that will not fade.

In your blue eyes, I see the future
like a river that flows and flows.
The rapids past, it now runs smoother
in closeness that grows and grows.

In your blue eyes, I see the grandeur
of all that was and is to be.
In your true love, I find a savior
from limits to eternity.

James and Carol

My troubadours you are the kings.
Your magic words in my mind ring
with simple truths to which I cling,
Carolina James, Carol King.

James' music in nostalgic strain
plays my dreams just like a guitar.
In words that speak of fire and rain
with melancholy's sweet memoir.

Carol plays, her piano sings
of love, girl groups and summer flings.
Tapestry of time she weaves
the summer's end and falling leaves.

It's nice to spend some time with you.
Some fleeting moments from my past.
And childhood dreams that might hold true
but growing old, they seldom last.

Jimmy Lai

Remember Jimmy Lai
who would not say goodbye?
Sentenced to jail for years
by China's cold oppressive fears.

Arrived without a cent.
Success was his intent.
Free press he did procure
and didn't remain obscure.

A humble Hong Kong guy.
He fought for liberty.
The lie he would deny
that Hong Kong is still free.

Free speech is what he sought.
Oppression what he fought.
Now locked away in jail
without a chance of bail.

Joy

Joy's a life preserver
that keeps us all afloat
in dark and stormy sea
when we tumble off the boat.

Joy's a rainbow's promise
of a new and perfect day;
reflected drops of dew
that shine in every way.

Joy: expectancy of good
like on a Christmas day;
a gift from our creator
that will forever stay.

We know that joy's not bought
nor earned. It shines from deep within.
Holy birthright, given
erasing grief or sin.

Joy is Love's pure music,
a symphony of good.
God plays in angel thoughts
praising Her Motherhood.

Like Tired Children

Pushed, the toddler fell. What a shock.
He hit his sister with a block.
Then she, upset, began to cry
and tried to poke him in the eye.

Their mother scooped them in her arms
to keep her children safe from harm;
tenderly put them in her bed.
"Sweet dreams and love," was all she said.

Lavender

In my daydream, I find Provence,
the south of France, the waves and sea.
A place where I was happy once.

My memory can take me there,
this magic place I long to be.
I fly on carpet through time's air

on winds which purple flowers blow
to crest like waves on surreal sea
in mauvish painting by Van Gogh.

The mustard house in distance calls
with red tile roof and wooden door.
I must be there before night falls.

The evening breeze will cast its spell
like Circe's call to distant shore.
Bewitched I fall into sweet smell

of lavender; this quiet queen
who reigns in paintings of Renoir.
Those paintings so much like my dream.

This flower's smell enchants the south's
serenity that I adore
like floral wine inside my mouth.

Calmness of this violet light
soothes me on time's pale purple shore
and ever will be my delight.

Love Remains
(Twenty years ago, 9/11)

We saw the worst in them
bring out the best in us.
Let's not remember hate.
but celebrate our love.

Those who fought and died that day
did not set out to be heroes.
Still, they didn't hesitate to act,
selflessly answered duty's call.

From falling dust our lives rebuilt
like towers of hope reaching up
with courage for brick and mortar,
and a great love designing all.

We proved the love in us
overcame hate in them.
Now, twenty years later,
Love is what still remains.

Luminaries

They are the lights that burn so bright,
salvation's beacons in the night.
The deep insight in what they write
will wed us to infinity.

In poetry, prose, or song
they lift us up where we belong.
They make us humble, make us strong,
and wed us to infinity.

These beacons, harbingers of good,
show us the way in which we should
free our small minds from all falsehood,
and wed us to infinity.

Shining like stars in sky above,
they give wisdom a needed shove.
They speak to us the truth they love,
and wed us to infinity.

Maria
(Maria Bethânia, Brazilian singer)

Come sing me a song, Maria
of distant land cross balmy seas;
your vocals float soft on the breeze.

Come sing me a song, Maria.
Your sultry voice my memories tease
and bossa notes my heartstrings' squeeze.

Come sing me a song, Maria.
Your music calls from sunlit keys
where I once found myself with ease.

Moving Out

My son moved out the other day.
In a strange way he did not say
he needed more space, but I knew.
His brother had gone long before
this other one walked out the door.

I knew for he was never home.
He did not want to be alone
with us, living with mom and dad.
He spent so much time with his friends
We never saw him in the end.

Now he has his very own place
With bedroom and basement space.
He's working hard to make it right
often he asks us to stop by.
We see more of him and that's why,

Moving's made all the difference.

Moonlight and Memory

Claire de Lune so softly sounds.
It floats across the twilit sky.
I clutch these notes of memory,
my fingers in my dad's palm lie.

I know with Dad, I am secure.
It is an evening long ago
and Dad once more walks by my side
in neighborhoods I used to know.

We slowly stroll cross Prospect Park
And when the concert ends, is done,
Dad's voice, a caress in the dark.
His only words, "I love you son."

My Woodpecker Friend

Thump, thump, thump upon my roof.
He lets me know it's not bug proof.
Jackhammer piercing wood or rock
wakes me like my alarm clock.

Bang, bang, bang goes the rapid fire
taking out bugs that he desires.
Like some soldier on foreign shore,
workman putting nails in a door.

I wake and chase him far away.
Then he returns another day.
He is a very loyal pest
but I would like to get some rest.

Notre Dame is Burning

Long hast thou stood "O church of God"
Christ's resurrection proclaiming.
More than building of wood and stone,
you are sacred life sustaining.

No fire can burn you, place of God.
We hold you safe in memory.
Nothing can kill our risen Christ.
A church of God once more you'll be.

Octopus Limbs

Last night I dreamt of octopus limbs.
The tentacles entwined my mind.
and when I hacked them to pieces
like some infected horrid vine,

they soon grew back like limbs of trees
or claws of an ungodly crab.
Could I escape this nightmare dream
created in some far flung lab?

One shot, another, make it three,
a booster's now just what you need.
One variant comes then another
just like returning demon seed.

Ode to Tolerance

Cancel me, then I'll cancel you.
In this new world, that's what we do.
Like female mantis eats her spouse
new culture will invade our house.

Others' views are now called bad.
No tolerance, it seems so sad
when persecution makes us glad
and past mistakes, a new launch-pad.

The Jacobins were zealots pure.
No opposition could endure
their reign of terror; that's for sure.
Today we call it our new cure.

Just think like us, you will survive.
Bow down. Give in. No compromise.
Others' views we marginalize,
cancel, ignore, or ostracize.

If we could only just agree
to treat each other with respect,
our fellow man then we would see
as brothers we could all accept.

Paris, Summer 1975

I sit by the Seine, sad, alone
In a city far from my home.
Exiled in country not my own
with no *petite amie* to phone.

Where have they gone, *les jeunes filles*?
Where are they now, what do they see
these erstwhile friends, *ma joie, ma vie*?
They loved me once, only to flee.

Poetry Reading

At the day's poetry reading
Echoes of the audience pleading,
clapping to show their approval,
anonymity's removal.

Pretending they now understand
the poem in the poet's hand.
Their sense of self is justified
They leave with ego satisfied.

Poet's Lament

If I could put my life in verse
and thus assure my place in time,
I'd sell my soul for all it's worth
to write a short melodic line.

For I have not the wit nor style
to hold my readers for a while.
To bind them with my words' caress
and break these walls of loneliness.

Rain Day

Something about a rainy day
when we take time to think or play.
No need for rain to go away.
The patter of the rain can stay.

On windows behind which I hide
the droplets, tears from heaven's eyes,
tell me in them I can confide,
in solitude we all abide.

The calm that comes on rainy days
without the sun and all its rays
can change our lives in many ways.
Our quest for quietness conveys.

Rebirth
(Ode to Charles d'Orleans)

The scent of spring is in the air.
The winter winds will soon have left.
And all the earth will bloom so fair
For we have had enough of death.

Resurrection Dawn

Day dawns in morning's mellow light
that needs not fight the dark of night.
Shadows dissolve, make radiant room
for those who rise from slumber's tomb.

We shield our eyes, the day so bright.
Then when accustomed to the sight
we step outside, re-clothed in white,
Timeless as Life, new as Christ.

Rhythm of Spirit

When we, made of heavenly light,
dance to the tune of holiness,
in rhythm with the universe,
the sons of God will shout for joy.
This earthly dance will disappear
and morning stars will sing.

Saul and Paul

Don't try so hard to win this race,
to merit what Paul called God's grace.
Human effort won't take the prize.
The crown is ours, just realize,

God's given his love to you.

Saul lived blind in his creed and law.
Love showed Paul what he'd missed before.
He ran the race, and with God's grace
He found the prize that he looked for.

Secret Garden

Inside this townhouse garden wall,
   a paradise of Verdean green,
the bashful chipmunk comes to call.
He searches for seeds not yet seen.

Bluebirds land on hanging feeders
   enjoying misty morning light.
These cheerful choral creatures,
are nature's gifts, my soul's delight.

If life were like this secret space
where birds with chipmunks thrive in peace,
we'd all commune with nature's grace.
dark days would fade, and war would cease.

Sentinel

I am the soldier at the gate.
Night has fallen, the hour is late.
My orders to keep all from harm,
stay alert and sound the alarm.

I stand against terror's attack.
My comrades know I have their back.
They know we all our promise keep
and if I die, they will not weep,

My mission's been to keep us free
and loyal soldiers all are we.
We'll meet in heaven down the hall
for faithful comrades are we all.

Sepia and Gold

The faded photograph was brown,
the frame of gilded gold.
The color of the couple's clothes
in thought I saw unfold.

Female Victorian velvet top
and matching floor-length skirt.
Bow at her throat and starched white blouse
Possessed of noble birth.

She stood, he sat, holding a child
dressed in shiny panache.
The father, bowtie, collared shirt
looked suave but somewhat brash.

The reddish tint stamped them in time
locked in their golden cage.
So lost in dreams that never age
on their gilded stage.

Shadow Warrior

His life lies in obscurity.
He cannot live like you and me.
A price he pays to keep us free.

A warrior on hidden field
his secrets are his sword and shield.
He cannot speak, his lips are sealed.

Player in game of global chess
he fights at his country's behest.
He has no time or place to rest.

When the fight is finally done,
the nation saved and we have won,
he tells his story to no one.

Shard of Time

Tatter of time torn from my mind,
a ragged edge, a shard of glass
reflecting faded shred of time
from shattered whole, that was the past.

Is it real, the pain I feel,
when microscope of memory
enlarges moments time concealed
creating now mad reverie?

A wisp of time is all I find,
the rest has gone, faded away.
I'd like to think that I was fine
when on that day she walked away.

Ships of Light
(Nautilus)

We take the polar lights for clothes.
The energy of Soul then shines
within our sailor-hearts and minds.

Pure pink and green, then yellow mix
the colors swirl round new forms.
Within is peace there are no storms.

Not Nemo sunk in waters deep
nor Lucifer for whom we weep.
Awaken from this earthly sleep!

When made anew in brilliant bliss
we dance to tune of holiness,
in rhythm with the universe.

Sleepwalk
(Santo and Johnny, 1959, "Sleepwalk")

Music inspired, they all slow danced
partners held close. "Sleepwalk" played on.
Teen lovers moved round the gym floor.
Bright dreams real, who'd ask for more.

Pre-teen I watched in silent wonder,
as the dancers swayed back and forth.
First kisses, tasted in my mind
hoping my true love, I would find.

The song's sad chords mirrored my thought
tugging at my lonely heartstrings
promised a dream I was too young
to catch. I clung to it, undone.

And as I turned and walked away
the music followed down the hall
haunting, teasing my preteen soul
With growing desire to be whole.

Songs in the Night

As darkness falls the monsters come.
Not ogres nor dragons that make me numb.
I wish they were just as unreal.
Then it might change the way I feel.

The worries that tomorrow brings
drift in and out of my strange dreams.
I toss and turn, then pop awake.
Will I now sleep before daybreak?

The moon and stars a symphony.
If I could feel, if I could see
this world is larger than just me.
Then I could rest, I could just be.

The glories of these jewel-crowned spheres
turn now my thoughts from selfish fears
and as I focus on its light
I hear their love-songs in the night.

Sunlight in Her Hair

She was his Venus in blue jeans,
a girl with sunlight in her hair.
In his fairytale world
No real girl could compare.

The years passed by, he gave up hope,
abandoned the vision it seems.
Till one day when he met her,
the woman of all his dreams.

Golden hair fell on her shoulders
Sunlight sparkled in her hair.
Years passed; her hair now gray
but still beyond compare.

On a late autumn eve, they sit
she and he, magic in the air;
his Venus in blue jeans
the answer to his prayer.

The Autocrats

Sometimes you find them on the Right
They are the keepers of the light
who ask for you to rise and fight
for Motherland and what is white.

At times, you find them on the Left.
The workers serve at their behest
for they always know what is best.
A better world is their great quest.

They both say:

Lend us support. Help take power.
Now is the time. Now is the hour.
But don't despair when all turns sour.
Under us you'll learn to cower.

If with us, you should disagree
then take your things, you need to flee.
For in our care, you can't be free.
Just say goodbye to liberty.

The Ides of March

In icy rain the redbuds show
their pretty pink, though down below
the lake is still, but cold winds blow.

As silent spring now dips her feet
in lake's new birth, winter's retreat,
the Ides of March will bring their sleet.

Just yesterday, I had in view
few daffodils were pushing through
before this spell of cold came new.

But icy rain and sleet can't kill
this sign of spring. On windowsill
the birds still perch and eat their fill.

Like harbingers of hope they sit.
A song of Spring they will permit.
And in my mind, a fire is lit.

Although the Ides of March will shun
the flower's bloom and newborn sun
a path to Spring will surely come.

The Summer of Our Discontent

The year is 1964: the summer of our discontent.
Piling into a blue station wagon,
hoping to redefine America by vote,
three activists disappear in Mississippi.

"When I get back, we'll go out for pizza,"
one activist tells his young brother.
He and the others do not come back.
Three activists disappear in Mississippi.

The attorney general sends the FBI.
White shirts and skinny black ties comb thickets,
finding a burnt station wagon left in a swamp.
Three activists disappear in Mississippi.

In the "deep bosom" of the earth buried,
hand with a ring, a bullet-torn torso
deformed, unfinished, sent before their time.
Three activists disappear In Mississippi.

The year is 1968, *The dogs bark* but we *march on to freedom*.
*We will not be judged by the color of our skin
but by the content of our character.* For this
three activists disappeared in Mississippi.

Another summer of discontent, 2021.
We continue, oppressed and oppressors.
And the sacrifices made in Mississippi?
Still judged by the color of our skin.

Transformation

Something is buried deep inside us
waiting to be revealed.
Like butterfly wings unfolding.

Yearning transformed into learning.
Reaching for light, ready to shine.
Not new birth, but revelation

like song as yet unsung,
patiently waiting for us to
learn and practice the tune.

Our voice rings forth strong, free.
We sing this song of liberty,
with wings unfurled for flight.

The Line

He waited in the long queue,
Afghan interpreter, true.
Airport and his plane in view,
he didn't have the slightest clue

what to do to get through
to the life he'd pursue.
City of light had gleamed,
called to him when he dreamed.

From his dream he was barred.
Alas, he had no green card.

There Be Dragons

Below them ran a wooden bridge
that crossed the river to the south.
The boy could see it from the ridge
some distance from the river's mouth.

"Don't cross the bridge, stay here with me."
Said his father on the knoll.
"There're dragons on the other side,
who breath fire. They will steal your soul."

"I want to see what's over there,"
the boy exclaimed with hope in heart.
The man replied, "My son beware.
They've fought us from the very start."

"Perhaps I'll like them; they'll like me,"
the boy replied, then shook his head.
"I want to talk to them, be free
to listen, ponder what is said."

"You will be changed, never return.
They'll brainwash you, that's what they'll do.
There's nothing from them you can learn.
You'll think like them and hate us too."

The boy felt sorry for the man
Who it seemed could not understand.
He stepped out on the wooden bridge.
then said as he waved at the ridge,

"If I can know them as they are
and in new friendships now succeed
then you can never go too far
to make an enemy a friend indeed."

Watchtowers of the Mind

Along watchtowers in my mind
I stand against the coming night.
Though terrors rush in, undefined
I will not yield without a fight.

By day I rest and wake at night
To walk mind's bulwarks, sound alarms.
I let the signal fires burn bright,
thought's sentinels, a call to arms.

There is no way I bow or yield
to nightmares, future or past.
Against these hordes, my will is steeled
till daylight brings me peace at last.

What If?

What if tomorrow's not the same
and I don't find that job?
What if it brings heartache and pain
or my knees start to throb?

"What is God's will for us?"
Eternal good alone for sure.
In Him we can forever trust.
And know our future is secure.

As we now face each coming day
There's only one way we can pray.
What we now need to say
is "Thank you, God, that we're okay."

We are the United States of America

"Don't worry my friend,"
the U.S. soldier said.
"You do not need to dread.
Just stand with us. Don't be misled."

"Don't worry my daughter,"
the father said. "Go to school.
There's no more Jihad rule.
You have a right to learn."

"We have a right to learn,"
the daughter boldly said
before the Taliban shot her dead.
They put a bullet in her head.

And as she fell her only thought,
if this is now the end,
I did not kneel or bend.
But where's the American friend?

A Friend

What is a true and loyal friend?
Someone who's there until the end,
travels with us a common road
and shares our often-heavy load.

Extending hand with comfort's art
can cheer us on, uplift our heart.
With healing balm help us to mend.
That is a true and loyal friend.

A Pirate's Life

Islet of the Bahamian sphere
midst a world so emerald blue
much sailed by pirate buccaneers
where overhead the white gulls flew.

The island had fresh water there
but food to eat did not come cheap.
We buccaneers did not despair
and dove for treasures of the deep.

Our hardy crew had lots of fruit
we mixed with rum and grenadine.
Like pirates fighting over loot
we cooked the concha meat in steam.

A moments treasure in the sun
then floating in the azure deep.
For even pirates must have fun
before they fall in mid-day sleep.

We boarded ship at end of day,
set sail upon the blue-green sea
and left behind the tranquil bay,
the setting sun a tapestry

of gold and orange harmony.
For this is how one's life should be
just softly floating on the sea.
The pirate's life's the one for me.

Arrowhead

There were three of us, explorers
scaling Indian mountain
which was our name for the boulder
that sat in the woods down the road.

I, being the oldest, was first
to reach to the summit
where we made our fort of timber,
protection against hostiles.

We had seen it all before on TV.
The cowboys and Indians
where white was good, and red was bad;
seventh cavalry died with boots on.

That day, we found an arrowhead
among pebbles and dust
atop our rock. A prize treasure.
Proof Indian tribes had existed.

As I think back with some fondness
it's mixed with great sadness
at the way we looked at the past,
how we bought the lies they sold on TV.

A Tree is a Tree
(A poem for the children)

A tree's always a tree.
That's what it's made to be.
It grows with light, though out of sight,
That's what it's made to be.

We are just like a tree.
Made perfect, you and me.
Being a child is key
To fuller life, you'll see.

We can never go far
from whom and what we are,
what He made us to be,
children of God and free.

World's End

Red sun sets, then sleeps.
Purple mountains sit silent.
Will tomorrow come?

ABOUT THE AUTHOR

Christian Pascale was a writer and a poet who was born in Brooklyn, New York. He graduated from Lafayette College Magna Cum Lauda with degrees in French and International Relations. At Lafayette, he was inducted into the Phi Beta Kappa honor society and then went on to receive an M.A. in European Area Studies from American University in Washington D.C. and a Doctorat de l'université from La Sorbonne in Paris, France. During his early years, he worked as a substitute teacher, a tennis instructor in Europe and the U.S., a teacher of English as a Foreign Language, a political fundraiser, and Director of Studies at a New England preparatory school. For more than thirty years, he worked in both domestic and foreign assignments for the United States Government.

Christian published twenty poems in two internationally distributed magazines and was a member of the James City Poets. His work can be found at christianpascale.com.

www.ingramcontent.com/pod-product-compliance
Lightning Source LLC
Chambersburg PA
CBHW012107090526
44592CB00019B/2679